Teacher's M

Getting Started in Theatre

Teacher's Manual

Getting Started in
Theatre

Linda Pinnell

National Textbook Company
a division of *NTC Publishing Group* • Lincolnwood, Illinois USA

Cover photographs: Dawn Murray, Theater and Interpretation Center
Northwestern University, Evanston, Illinois

Published by National Textbook Company, a division of NTC Publishing Group.
© 1995 by NTC Publishing Group, 4255 West Touhy Avenue
Lincolnwood (Chicago), Illinois 60646-1975 U.S.A.
All rights reserved. No part of this book may be reproduced, stored
in a retrieval system, or transmitted in any form or by any means,
electronic, mechanical, photocopying, recording or otherwise, without
prior permission of NTC Publishing Group.
Manufactured in the United States of America.

4 5 6 7 8 9 0 VP 9 8 7 6 5 4 3 2 1

CONTENTS

About the Student Edition		vii
Chapter One	What Is Drama?	1
Chapter Two	Types of Drama	3
Chapter Three	Setting the Scene	7
Chapter Four	Characterization Through Costumes and Makeup	11
Chapter Five	The Actor's Role	15
Chapter Six	Movement and Improvisation	19
Chapter Seven	Voice and Interpretation	23
Chapter Eight	The Director's Responsibility	25
Chapter Nine	From Audition to Performance	27
Chapter Ten	Selected Scenes for Acting Practice	29
Resource Lists for Theatre Educators		31
Performance, Activity, and Evaluation Forms: Blackline Masters		37

ABOUT THE STUDENT EDITION

This text, *Getting Started in Theatre*, serves as an introduction to the complex world of theatre.

Its goals are as follows:

1. To help students understand what drama is and how it differs from other literary forms.
2. To introduce students to the common forms of drama, offering them a historical overview.
3. To briefly explain to students the most basic aspects of set design, lighting, and stage props.
4. To show students how costumes and makeup aid in the portrayal of a character.
5. To expose students to various theories of acting.
6. To provide students with experiences and insights about stage movement.
7. To encourage students to experiment with vocal interpretation.
8. To clarify for students the director's role in a production.
9. To show students the rehearsal process from start to finish.
10. To offer students opportunities for acting practice through a wide variety of scenes from classical and contemporary dramas.

Organization and Use of the Text

Getting Started in Theatre is designed as text for a one-semester introductory theatre course, as well as a supplement for an English or communications course in which drama and theatre are treated in a four to six week unit. Many English classes study pieces of drama but often fail to discuss or do activities that clarify how these pieces transfer from page to stage, thus failing to acknowledge the true purpose of the form.

In addition to the information presented, each chapter gives activities that involve the students in drama as performance rather than as literature. Many of these activities are adaptable as homework or writing assignments, but many really require students to become physically involved in ways that simulate and establish a performance environment. The course length will probably determine how much attention you choose to devote to the activities.

Other Suggestions for Use

1. The text is divided into ten chapters. Each of the first nine deals with a specific aspect of theatre; the last gives a variety of scenes that may be used for practice in interpretation. You may choose to deal with particular chapters as they become relevant to you (for example, costuming and stagecraft as you are preparing for a production). However, the chapters interlock to give a general overview of theatre.

2. Each chapter may serve as a one-night homework assignment, or you may wish to develop a chapter into a major unit. For example, do you want the students to read about makeup one day and watch one brief demonstration, or have the opportunity to experiment with applying stage makeup over a period of days?
3. Students may use *Getting Started in Theatre* to imagine how a play they are reading in English class would transfer to the stage. On the other hand, they may read it as part of their preparation for mounting an actual production of the play.
4. Students may watch a college, community, or professional performance and then analyze it in terms of the various production aspects they have read about. It may be helpful to bring in guest speakers associated with these productions to allow students to ask specific questions about the performances.
5. The scenes included in Chapter Ten may be used as exercises for vocal interpretation, blocking, or actual performance. These activities may be expanded to accommodate specific teaching situations or to serve as a springboard to independent projects.
6. This text provides a constant emphasis on the production aspect of theatre. Whether students are reading plays in English class or planning to perform them in a theatre department, they should have an understanding of why the writer chose to present ideas in this genre, rather than in a novel, short story, or poem.

Chapter One: What Is Drama?

OUTCOMES

After completing this chapter, the student will

1. Appreciate drama as a performance art rather than just a literary form.
2. Appreciate how the oral tradition and the human desire to "playact" combine in the genre of drama.
3. Understand the evolution of drama from a religious ritual to an entertainment phenomenon.
4. Understand the appeals of and differences between various types of drama.
5. Understand how certain themes and characters from literature have persisted and evolved throughout the history of theatre.

SUGGESTIONS FOR TEACHING

This chapter is an overview of theatre history. It emphasizes the constant evolution of theatre throughout history and the innate need in people to share stories in performance before an audience.

At all times help students develop the awareness of activities they have observed or been involved in as elemental forms of theatre. You will note that most activities in this chapter are geared toward discussion. Most could also be structured as writing assignments. In this chapter, only one is structured as a performance activity. Performance activities will become more numerous in later chapters as students lose inhibitions and gain confidence.

Activity One

Your teacher will divide the class...all were talented, dramatic storytellers....

Even students who believe they have had no contact with theatre have been exposed to some of its elemental concepts. Reading aloud and storytelling are very much performance arts for which most students have been eager audience members. However, many students have never analyzed specific elements such as facial expression, vocal variety, and gesture as attributes of a good storyteller. When they listen to speakers with these specific ideas in mind, it will become easier for them to identify these qualities. Although this is a performance activity, its initial phase takes place in the relative safety of a small-group setting, which will allow even inhibited students to participate. Since the best storytellers will probably be the less inhibited students, they will no doubt be the first ones to perform in front of the entire class. This activity will serve as an icebreaker for future performance activities.

Activity Two

What was your favorite game of pretending...a battlefield?

This activity once again emphasizes that even those students who believe they have had no theatre experience have indeed engaged in some elements of theatre. Most students have in their past a history of pretending to be another person—theatre minus the audience. This activity also emphasizes that many elements of theatre, such as costumes and props, are a natural outgrowth of the attempt to portray characters in another reality. This is one of those activities that could be adapted into a writing exercise.

Activity Three

Brainstorm for a minute...what would you do?

In this high-tech age, many students feel that theatre, like film, is enhanced by, if not dependent upon, special effects. This activity emphasizes that during good times and bad times throughout history, theatre has flourished. It also shows students that there are ways to compensate for the less than ideal facilities they may encounter in school and community auditoriums. In short, this activity should prove that theater can exist and thrive in many different settings.

Activity Four

What is your all-time favorite movie..."tear jerkers"?

Some ancient concepts such as catharsis, which date back to the time of Aristotle, may seem foreign to the modern theatre student. Through an examination of the appeal of the modern "tear jerker," students should come to a better understanding of Aristotle's term and its relationship to tragedy.

Activity Five

Certain one-dimensional characters from early comedy...the pretentious scholar.

It is easy for students to assume that what is new to them is totally original. It is important to realize that, especially in comedy, many styles of theatre are derivatives of earlier forms. This activity emphasizes stock characters and familiar scenarios but also provides a springboard for discussion of revivals, remakes, and updates of classic plays and movies.

Chapter Two: Types of Drama

OUTCOMES

After completing this chapter, the student will

1. Understand what sets drama apart from other forms of literature.
2. Be able to define and differentiate between the most common forms of drama.
3. Understand the interplay between various forms of drama.
4. Be able to identify dramatic conventions such as *monologue, soliloquy,* and *aside*, and understand why they are useful in the development of a play.
5. Understand that no matter what length or act structure an author uses, all drama is based on conflict that follows an identifiable pattern of building action, climax and resolution.

SUGGESTIONS FOR TEACHING

This chapter is mainly informational, so it may be especially appropriate for homework or independent reading. Much of it is devoted to definitions that will help students distinguish among various forms of drama. This ability to analyze the playwright's intent will be helpful later in exercises involving acting and play production.

THE DUAL NATURE OF COMEDY AND TRAGEDY

In trying to label plays, students often fail to realize how often comedy and tragedy overlap and how fine the line between these two seeming opposites actually can be. Point out that skilled writers like Shakespeare often interspersed scenes of comic relief within the tensest moments of a tragedy. It may be helpful for them to see how the porter's scene in *Macbeth* or the gravedigger's scene in *Hamlet* allows the audience to catch their breath before the tension begins to build again.

Activity One

Do you have a "tragic flaw"...Write a brief scenario....

For many students there is no distinction between sad and tragic. In drama, there is a difference. Although the typical student may not meet the ancient qualifications for a tragic hero, most students can relate to the concept of the tragic flaw, that disturbing personality trait that may have kept them from attaining their goals. Since the admission of a tragic flaw is sometimes rather difficult, this may lend itself to a written assignment. In this way, the student can put more honest thought into the problem of the tragic hero and how the tragic flaw affects the character's circumstances.

THE COMIC DIFFERENCE

Many find comedy easier to recognize than to define, probably because a person's sense of humor is so individual.

The sections that follow explain the general concepts of comedy and drama and distinguish some of the more familiar types.

Activity Two

What is your favorite TV show?...prove this.

It is easier to make judgments than it is to analyze them. Most students can tell you their favorite TV show but may be hesitant to label a soap opera as melodrama or a situation comedy as farce because these labels have taken on negative connotations outside their dramatic contexts. When students are forced to defend their chosen shows with specific examples of plotting, dialogue, and characterization, these labels become clearer.

Activity Three

As a class or in small groups...typify each category defined.

This activity expands upon Activity Two. Since some students may watch only sitcoms or soap operas, they may have problems finding examples of other types of drama. The input from other class members is helpful in putting together a broader pool of viewing experiences.

PRESENTATIONAL AND REPRESENTATIONAL

Going back to what theatre critic and author Alexander Bakshy first labeled as presentational and representational may help students understand the dynamics of how an actor relates to an audience. In a realistic play, one of the biggest problems a fledgling actor confronts is holding his or her concentration on the play rather than the audience. Conversely, many beginning actors find it hard to "play" the audience in a less realistic show. This distinction may be helpful in determining the proper level of involvement with the audience called for by the style of the play.

In addition, this section discusses three conventions of dramatic speech: the monologue, the soliloquy, and the aside. While most students have few problems with dialogue, these more contrived elements frequently elude them in silent reading and often even in reading aloud. In addition to the definitions, excerpts from three well-known plays are presented.

If you wish to refer students to the movie *Ferris Bueller's Day Off*, in terms of presentational style, note that it is on videotape.

CONFLICT

No piece of literature can exist without conflict. This is especially true in drama for the theatre; the audience cannot walk away from a play and come back two hours later as they may with a novel. Students need to understand how conflict provides the framework of the play. They also need to understand the various types of conflict that authors work with. It may be helpful for students to diagram familiar plays to see how playwrights introduce, build, and resolve conflict.

Chapter Three: Setting the Scene

OUTCOMES

After completing this chapter, the student will

1. Understand the importance of setting on the characters and events of a play.
2. Be able to identify various types of stages and understand the production advantages and disadvantages special to each one.
3. Be able to identify the acting areas of a conventional stage.
4. Understand how set, lighting, and props contribute to creating the world of the play.
5. Know enough about various technical aspects of setting to analyze them from either an audience or a stage crew perspective.

TEACHING SUGGESTIONS

Everything that is discussed in this chapter is worthy of its own volume. The information and activities here form a good starting point for learning some very basic things about set design, lighting, and props. If your students are actually going to build flats or set lights, there are many good books that discuss technical and safety aspects in great detail. Some of these are listed in the bibliography and resource list in the student text.

Activity One

Read the following scene carefully...#1: Oh... #2: I will...

This Open Scene activity was originally conceived by Wandalie Henshaw as an exercise in directing. The scene, and the accompanying article, appeared in the October 1969 issue of *Educational Theater Journal*. Although it was initially geared to directors and may prove an interesting directing exercise for students later in the semester, it is used here because there is no specific identification of characters or setting. These lines are subject to any number of interpretations. Students may simply analyze these scenes or they may pair off and present their varying interpretations to the class.

Activity Two

Imagine that you were going to write an autobiographical play...

Students must get beyond thinking of characters as cardboard creations. This exercise forces the student to transform himself or herself into a character of sorts, and to develop settings which reveal the character's personality. After working through this activity, discuss with students how this process carries over to the surroundings of fictional people.

TYPES OF STAGES

Before students can begin to think in terms of scene design, they must understand the various work areas. Since the stage directions given in most scripts are written for a proscenium stage, it is easy for students to assume all stages are interchangeable. It is very important that students understand the basic concepts involved in staging and be able to identify the three types of stages.

Activity Three

Using the guidelines given for identifying the three types of stages...

It is one thing to understand diagrams of the types of stages; it is another to be able to identify them when you actually see them. Besides the school auditorium, students have probably been to plays, pageants, and concerts in other venues. In addition to classifying the various stages they are familiar with, discuss with students the types of performances they have attended and why the settings were effective or ineffective for those particular events. If possible, let the class talk to people who have directed, designed, or acted in these settings about the specific advantages and problems encountered there.

TYPES OF SETS

The more plays students have a chance to see, the more familiar they will be with the wide range of setting options. This section explains some of the basic types of sets, but nothing can substitute for seeing the actual thing assembled, both from the audience and from backstage if possible. The best alternative to numerous field trips to local and regional productions is to invest in a few good scene design books that show a variety of completed sets and explain their construction.

Activity Four

Choose a play from the library...modify this for a less elaborate setting.

By this time students should be very familiar with the stage area that will be the site of their future productions. They should have discussed in detail the pitfalls of that particular stage area. Now comes the decision that any director and set designer really must make: Is the play adaptable to the particular venue, and what staging concessions have to be made for it to work? Let students present their solutions to staging problems. Give special praise to creative solutions.

LIGHTING

Lighting may be the area where, for at least the first few productions, you are most limited by your technical capabilities and your facilities. Before investing in new equipment, you will probably want to call upon someone with real expertise to help you determine what new instruments will best suit your needs and what your wiring and electrical system will safely accommodate.

PROPS

Regardless of what type of staging is used, stage props are important. This section emphasizes that stage props must look historically accurate, be durable enough to withstand rehearsal and performance, and be easy for the actors to work with. Students need to realize that props must be well thought-out. Props—or at least temporary substitute props—are some of the first items to be added to a rehearsal process, so students on a property crew must be especially reliable and attentive to detail.

Activity Five

Using the same play you chose for scene design, make a list of all props...

When a play is well-produced, it is easy to imagine that the world on stage came completely preassembled. This activity forces students to think about where every prop on stage actually comes from. Since many of these props cannot be readily acquired, they must be constructed, which presents another challenge to the property crew. Really pin students down on what they have in the *Borrow* and *Construct* columns. *Will* you be able to borrow these items? How and of what materials will the props be constructed? Give credit to truly creative solutions.

Chapter Four: Characterization Through Costumes and Makeup

OUTCOMES

After completing this chapter, the student will

1. Be able to visualize how a character dresses based upon what is given in the script.
2. Appreciate costuming as a way of not only defining characters but also establishing the historical context of a play.
3. Have some background on the development of costuming in the history of the theatre.
4. Be able to analyze what effect costume colors have on the image of a character.
5. Know what resources to consult for costume rental or construction information.
6. Understand the functions of stage makeup.
7. Practice designing and possibly applying makeup for a variety of characters.

TEACHING SUGGESTIONS

This chapter may be used as a classroom lesson or as a starting point for an actual theatrical production. You may wish to refer students to handbooks on costuming and makeup, such as those listed in the bibliography in the student text, for detailed information.

Activity One

Costume the following characters for a play...

Most students will insist that they do not stereotype by appearance, yet most are guilty of it. Rather than assess characters or people by their clothing, this exercise begins at the reverse point. Students are asked to costume "characters" about whom they know only one fact. Let students make notations, write a description or even sketch what these characters look like in costume. Afterward compare their impressions and note the similarities. It may be helpful to discuss where costuming stereotypes work effectively and where they may work against the production.

CHARACTER TYPES

Emphasize that some types of plays, such as the commedia del l'arte (Italian, *comedy of art*) rely on one-dimensional characters that the audience can immediately recognize. But it is also important that students realize that modern playwrights work with more complexity and subtlety. Point out that in the world of theatre there are few typical lawyers, typical police officers, or typical housewives, unless they are intentionally stereotyped for a certain effect.

Activity Two

Go back and choose one of those flat characters from Activity One...

After discussing when and why stereotypes do and do not work, let students choose one character to "round" into a more fully developed character. The focus here should be on how this individual differs from a generic English teacher or used-car salesman. After rounding out their characters, students may sketch the revised costume, or if there is time, students may even assemble and model the costume for the class.

COLOR

If possible, it might be fun to have a color consultant come in and talk about colors that flatter and distract from the individual. In addition (or in lieu of this activity), bring in swatches of fabric and let students decide what types of characters might be costumed in the assorted materials.

Activity Three

What do these color choices seem to reveal about...?

Aside from the simple idea of colors that are flattering to the individual, a costumer must be aware of the psychological and cultural implications of certain colors. Before beginning this exercise, it may be wise to discuss the symbolism of various colors in our culture and the way in which certain colors are perceived. Once you have established the impact of the colors themselves, translate them to specific articles of clothing.

THE COSTUME OR PERIOD SHOW

Students should realize that costuming as we know it is a relatively new phenomenon. However, when a production attempts to portray a certain historical period, it must be accurately costumed. There are excellent costume encyclopedias that look at general styles and trends of many historical periods. This discussion will become more relevant if you have students look at styles and fads of their own era and the eras of their parents and grandparents. Discuss how these styles developed. Which are based purely on fashion? Which are based on more practical considerations? Which are obvious efforts to emulate some cultural icon of the moment?

Activity Four

Choose a play from another time period...

This is a research-oriented activity, one that will show students how to locate ideas for shows from another era. Allow students to sketch or photocopy illustrations that they feel are appropriate for specific characters. Those students especially interested in costuming may find or develop a pattern for a costume. Some students may even opt to construct a costume.

MAKEUP

There will be two primary obstacles to overcome with stage makeup. Girls may assume it should look like street makeup; boys may believe only wimps wear it. Consequently, students need to see what stage makeup looks like up close and under stage lights. They also need to see how washed out an actor with no makeup looks under stage lights. If possible, set up these demonstrations *before* beginning a unit on makeup so that students understand its importance.

Activity Five

Decide how you would design makeup for...or actually do the makeup.

Most students can quickly become adept with "straight" makeup. Character makeup will provide more of a challenge. There are many excellent books that explain facial structure in detail. This is excellent for doing a makeup plot but does not substitute for experimentation. Every actor should know how to do his or her own basic old-age makeup, so it might be fun to actually practice this in class. The more fanciful designs may work best as demonstrations by more skilled students.

Chapter Five: The Actor's Role

OUTCOMES

After completing this chapter, the student will

1. Appreciate an actor's skill in creating a character using the "instrument" of voice and body.
2. Understand the concept of character "type" and how it may be limiting to an actor.
3. Be able to delve into a character and develop the empathy needed for its portrayal.
4. Be able to identify and differentiate between the two primary schools of acting and use elements of both in developing a character.

TEACHING SUGGESTIONS

Many successful actors and directors have written detailed texts on techniques of acting that may provide insights into every aspect of acting. The information provided here is very introductory in nature. Most classrooms will not become intensive studio workshops that teach one style of acting; therefore, activities here attempt to provide simple exercises to introduce students to different acting styles. From this point on, activities will be based on getting students up and moving, instead of reading and watching.

INTERPRETING A ROLE

It is easy for the first-time actor to become so caught up in learning lines and blocking that interpretation takes a backseat. You should emphasize to students that interpretation is what sets acting apart from flat recitation. Perhaps the easiest way to discuss this is through their own observations. Do any of them have a favorite novel they have seen adapted for the screen? Were there characters that didn't quite work on film, while others were fabulous? Point out how the actor's interpretation of the character either matched or clashed with theirs as a reader. From there, discuss the specifics of why the one performance fit exactly and why the other was disconcerting. How were these interpretations justified by the text of the novel?

CHARACTER TYPE

Just as readers love to put themselves in the stead of the heroes and heroines who bear little resemblance to themselves, so do actors love to play characters different from their own physical types. Still, every actor who auditions on a professional or amateur level must realize that, in terms of audience credibility, there is only so much an actor can do when working against physical type.

CHARACTER DEVELOPMENT

The transformation from the character on paper to the character on stage may seem like a mystical process that is easier for some actors than others. Still, there are factors to consider in aiding this transformation. Just as real people have reasons for their actions, so do fictional characters. It is up to the actor to discover this motivation and empathetically portray it to the audience. You may begin this discussion by looking at controversial actions of literary or historical figures and deciding what motivated these actions.

ACTING—THE TECHNICAL METHOD

Times change. Styles change. Nowhere is this more evident than in communications. Students should realize that the so-called technical method of acting traces its roots back to ancient Greek and Roman oratorical systems. Today, most of us are put off by a speaker who seems studied rather than spontaneous. Similarly, we respond negatively to an actor who seems too programmed. Although most acting classes today rely almost entirely on method acting, there are some techniques from the technical system which may enhance any actor's repertoire.

Activity One

Describe or enact the posture, facial expressions, and gestures you would associate with these situations...

Although the technical method seems so oratorical that it is an anachronism on the modern stage, there are some merits in its basic premises. For instance, students may not have experienced the death of a close friend or an important job interview. However, they probably are familiar with the physical cues that accompany the emotions in these situations and can draw upon them for line interpretation.

METHOD ACTING

There are many books that have been published about Stanislavski's "method," some of them written by Constantin Stanislavski (sometimes spelled Konstantin Stanislavsky) himself or by his famous disciple, Lee Strasberg. Given this fact, a brief unit on method acting is an acknowledged oversimplification. You may wish to refer students to the bibliography in the student text for more detailed research on acting.

Activity Two

What event from your past would you conjure up...so that you might successfully portray it on stage?

While quite simple, this exercise allows students to get in touch with the emotional triggers they might use to portray certain emotions. Since students are often reticent about sharing very personal, emotional experiences, this activity may be tricky. Instead of discussing what triggers students have used, let them enact one of these emotions in an improvised or written scene of their own choice.

Activity Three

Choose a contemporary figure or a figure from history or literature...

Often student actors have trouble with motivation when they themselves would have handled a situation differently from the way a character in a play does. However, when watching an actor, the audience must believe the character behaves for a legitimate reason. This first-person exercise forces students to examine moral codes and motivation from the character's point of view.

Chapter Six: Movement and Improvisation

OUTCOMES

After completing this chapter, the student will

1. Be aware of movement as a defining attribute of characterizaton, especially in terms of age, gender, physical condition, and personality.
2. Be aware of social norms and period dress as determinants of movement.
3. Practice movement appropriate to a variety of characters.
4. Become comfortable with the essential concept of pantomime and practice a variety of applications.
5. Understand the value of improvisation in providing spontaneity for an actor and experiment with improvisation based on a variety of characters and scenarios.

TEACHING SUGGESTIONS

This chapter is almost entirely activity-based, since no amount of discussion about physicalization or movement can ever substitute for the actual practice. It is important to provide an environment where students feel comfortable attempting these exercises without giving into that most paralyzing adolescent problem, the fear of looking stupid.

Activity One

Choose someone that you know personally...
There is often a sense of unreality about a character in a drama. For that reason it may be easier for students to begin by studying and analyzing the movements of people in real life. By noting how important these aspects are in assessing and describing a real person, it becomes easier to then translate them to the physicalization of a character being developed.

Activity Two

Adopt one of the following character types and walk across the stage as that character...
When developing a character, an actor picks up on many nuances. Obviously there is more to each of these characters than his or her walk, but it is a good starting point. In learning lines, student actors acknowledge that the characters speak words different from their own; but they often fail to realize that characters may stand and move in different ways too. This activity also gets students up on stage and moving in front of an audience.

FACTORS OF MOVEMENT

We are subconsciously aware of how people move, but may not stop to consider the specific elements of movement. Once again the emphasis is on avoiding the stereotypical caricature. Discuss the specific elements of gender, age, physical condition, and social norms in shaping a character's movement. As much as possible, incorporate students' observations of contemporary performers and classic performances into the discussion.

Activity Three

As a class put yourself in the following situations...

The previous exercise had students individually experimenting with character walks. This exercise allows those who are a little more inhibited to work in a group. After these exercises, point out where students naturally interacted with each other. Although much more structured, this same interaction takes place on stage, where actors must be aware of their colleagues' physical actions and react accordingly. Let those students who are observing note particularly realistic bits of business.

SENSE MEMORY

One of the most difficult skills for an actor to learn is pantomime. Most of the things actors are called upon to pantomime on stage are actions they have performed a hundred times, but now they have to rely upon the sense memory—the memory of what the action felt like. Whether an actor ever has to use pantomime on stage or not, it is a useful skill to have. It requires the actor to develop a sense of his or her own body in relation to the surrounding space and objects.

Activity Four

In small groups, perform the following activities in front of the class...

This exercise again allows for group interaction. Activity Three sets up some basic pantomime exercises. This activity goes beyond the situation and includes invisible props. Much of this exercise involves sense memory in terms of the dimensions and density of the various objects. Let the students experiment with pantomime situations. Then, if possible, get the actual objects to let students handle them. After this, run the exercise again, while the feel of the objects is fresh in the students' minds.

IMPROVISING DURING REHEARSAL

Although improvisation may seem to be the forte of commedia troupes and Second City alumni, it is a necessity for all actors. Many beginning actors go into rehearsal with the idea of memorized lines that will be delivered by rote. However, just as in real life, the stage often provides some unexpected twists and turns that require improvisation. Most importantly, improvisation forces actors to listen and respond to what is happening on stage at that moment, thus being prepared for the unexpected and keeping the acting fresh for each new audience.

Activity Five

Improvise one of the following situations in front of the class...

Just as important as being physically aware of the other actors is listening to them, being tuned in to everything that is going on in a scene. Since improvisation is always unpredictable, an actor cannot fall into the trap of rattling off memorized lines with no sense of living the scene for the first time. Improvisation helps overcome this problem and allows students to quickly develop characters and learn how a conflict builds to an eventual climax and resolution.

Students may even come up with more characters and scenarios for original improvisations, or they may move to improvising dialogue for familiar characters from novels and short stories.

Chapter Seven: Voice and Interpretation

OUTCOMES

After completing this chapter, the student will

1. Recognize voice as an essential part of characterization.
2. Be able to define and experiment with specific qualities of the voice such as pitch, tone, rate, and articulation.
3. Be aware of the importance of dialect in establishing a character's background.
4. Be able to choose and analyze a scene and then vocally interpret a character or characters from it.

TEACHING SUGGESTIONS

Although this chapter deals with vocal interpretation, it culminates with activities that allow students to use other skills too. It should be pointed out to students that some forms of theatre (oral interpretation, puppet theatre, radio, and voice-overs in animated film) rely entirely on the actor's voice.

QUALITIES OF THE VOICE

If possible, invite a voice coach, or a forensic team coach to talk to students. People tend to look at the qualities of the voice as being unalterable, without realizing that these qualities can be worked upon and improved or changed for a specific purpose. It is important for students to realize that the voice is a mechanism that can be fine-tuned and refined with proper motivation and hard work.

Activity One

Think about people you know personally or actors whose voices you hear frequently...

Most students don't realize the impact a voice has on our image of a person. Would Arnold Schwarzenegger be so appealing if he sounded like Elmer Fudd? This exercise asks the student to analyze familiar voices in terms of the personality traits they seem to convey. After carefully analyzing these voices, students should be able to come up with the qualities they want to develop in conveying a character's personality. Every student should have heard a tape recording of his or her natural voice by this time so that he realizes what the starting point is. Similarly, a tape recorder may be helpful in the rehearsal process while an actor is trying to find the right character voice.

Activity Two

Choose one of the following words or phrases. See how many interpretations...

Tone allows us to pick up on shades of meaning that mere words do not provide. The words may be the same, but do they reflect enthusiasm, disbelief, sarcasm, insincerity, or apathy? Let students experiment with how much they can say with these simple, everyday phrases while the rest of the class tries to identify the emotional content.

DIALECT

You may enlist the help of your foreign language teachers to point out that there are some vowel and consonant sounds unique to any language. These are the sounds that usually make learning a stage dialect more difficult.

Teachers should use discretion in this activity and encourage students to be sensitive to stereotypical portrayals.

Activity Three

Choose a dialect that you are familiar with...

Many students know at least one person with an identifiable dialect. The problem is that most have never analyzed exactly what vowel changes and consonant replacements make the dialect sound odd to them. This exercise helps students to focus specifically on the differences within a dialect and to try to reproduce it. Stress to students that the dialect should be accurate and should not be intended to make fun of someone who speaks in a different manner.

Chapter Eight: The Director's Responsibility

OUTCOMES

After completing this chapter, the student will

1. Recognize the director as the key to pulling the show together.
2. Be able to identify the wide variety of responsibilities the director takes on.
3. Understand the director's specific job in holding auditions, establishing the look and feel of the show, blocking the show, and conducting rehearsals.

TEACHING SUGGESTIONS

Since students should have considerable experience in acting and stagecraft before they are allowed to direct a real production, this chapter may seem less relevant than some of the others in an introductory text. However, it is important for students to realize that whether they are acting or working on a crew, they are ultimately responsible to one individual whose vision shapes the production. That individual is the director.

Activity One

Choose one of the scenes from Chapter Ten. Cast and block that scene...

Directing, like teaching, often looks deceptively easy. Students will be less likely to complain about a director after they have fulfilled that role themselves, even for a two- or three-page scene. This activity refers students to scenes in Chapter Ten, but you may wish to use other scenes.

You may decide to have students block the scenes on paper, then discuss specific blocking with them, or you may let them move real people around on stage to test their eye for blocking. Depending on the amount of time available, students could actually produce these scenes as playlets or performance pieces, complete with simple set, costumes, and props.

Chapter Nine: From Audition to Performance

OUTCOMES

After completing this chapter, the student will

1. Understand the rehearsal process.
2. Be aware of the commitments and responsibilities involved in the rehearsal period for a production.
3. Be able to trace the development of a production from script to production.
4. Have a basic understanding of the stages of the rehearsal process and its approximate time frame.

TEACHING SUGGESTIONS

Without an ongoing production, this chapter may seem to exist in a kind of limbo. However, it is a good introduction to the sequence of events and time frame of the rehearsal process, including the audition. This chapter is also a reminder that although being involved in a play is fun, it is a major time commitment and a lot of hard work.

Activity One

Choose a favorite novel or short story. Pretend that you are casting for the movie version...

Perhaps no aspect of the rehearsal process causes more consternation among students than auditions and these inevitable questions: Why didn't I get cast? Why didn't I get the role I wanted?

These may never be satisfactorily answered for every student, but letting students cast a favorite novel from a pool of film actors that they don't know personally may give them some insight into the process. From the ensuing discussion on their casting choices, it should become obvious that there are many factors that may influence casting, but personal favoritism is usually very low on the list.

Activity Two

Selecting a play you would want to perform, set up a rehearsal schedule...

You may refer students to the bibliography and resource list in the text for titles of plays for consideration, or you may recommend drama collections available in the classroom or library. Another option is to pre-select a few plays and offer them to your students. (See the resource list in this manual.) At this time, you should discuss the matters of obtaining performance rights and paying royalties, assuming some plays up for consideration may not be in the public domain. Posing a hypothetical situation, you may wish to have students explore how to go about getting permission to perform such plays in school or professional productions.

Students are often overwhelmed by the rehearsal process the first time they are involved in a play. This exercise allows students to see how, in a specific time frame, the director must keep adding new elements until the play progresses from script and cold auditions to the final polished production before an audience.

Chapter Ten: Selected Scenes

Several activities in the text refer students to this collection of scenes or cuttings for acting, interpretation, and directing practice. A variety of dramatic styles is presented, with playwrights ranging from Shakespeare to Susan Glaspell to David Henry Hwang. Some of these eleven scenes may be used for practice in dialect; all lend themselves to line interpretation, as well as to experimenting with blocking and stage movement.

For copyright and performance rights information on the plays from which these scenes are drawn, see the acknowledgments page in the student text, which notes information on those plays not in the public domain. For suggestions on other plays that may be studied or performed and general information on play production supply houses, see the resource list in the student text.

To assist you and your students in interpreting, performing, or directing the scenes in the text or other performance pieces, see the performance activity and evaluation forms at the end of this manual.

Resource Lists for Theatre Educators

SOURCES FOR PLAYS

The most important decision the producer or director makes is the choice of a script. If you don't have a vast knowledge of what's out there, especially more recent works, or if you have questions about royalties and other production considerations, the first step is building up a storehouse of play catalogs. These catalogs are published by the company that owns the rights to the plays they list.

The catalog listing for each play, similar to those in the resource list in *Getting Started in Theatre*, provides a brief blurb, telling you haw many actors—male and female—are required to cast the play; how many interior and exterior sets must be built; the date of the setting if it is an historical piece; and, a brief synopsis of the play. Although the catalog blurb gives enough information to know if the play is totally unfeasible for your group to produce, you cannot make a positive decision based on so little information. As the instructor or director of a school production, you may order reading scripts of several plays that sound promising and make your decision from there.

The following is a list of publishers who specialize in plays:

Anchorage Press, Inc.
P.O. Box 8067
New Orleans, LA 70182-8067

Art Craft Play Company
Box 1058
Cedar Rapids, IA 25406

Baker Plays
100 Chauncy Street
Boston, MA 02111

Contemporary Drama Service
Meriwether Publishing Co.
Box 7710
Elkton Drive
Colorado Springs, CO 80903

The Dramatic Publishing Co.
123 Sharp Hill Rd.
Wilton, CT 06897

Dramatists Play Service
440 Park Avenue South
New York, NY 10016

Eldridge Publishing Co.
P.O. Drawer 216
Franklin, OH 45005

Samuel French, Inc.
45 W. 25th Street
New York, NY 10010

Heuer Publishing Co.
Drawer 248
Cedar Rapids, IA 52406

Pioneer Drama Service
P.O. Box 22555
Denver, CO 80222

Players Press, Inc.
P.O. Box 1137
Studio City, CA 91614-0132

Playwrights Canada Press
Imprint of Playwrights Union of Canada
54 Wolseley Street
2nd Floor
Toronto, Ontario, M5T 1A5 Canada

SOURCES FOR MUSICALS

Music Theater International
119 W. 57th Street
New York, NY 10019

Tams-Witmark Music Library
757 Third Avenue
New York, NY 10017

Rodgers and Hammerstein Repertory
460 Park Avenue
New York, NY 10022

SOURCES FOR SUPPLIES

Two comprehensive theatre supply catalogs are available. Information about single copy and subscription rates is available from the address listed.

The New York Theatrical Sourcebook. Available from Broadway Press, 120 Duane Street, #407, New York NY 10007. (This volume lists 2,500 companies who provide materials and services for the stage. It contains a listing of companies providing special effects items and machines.)

Theatre Crafts Annual Directory. Available from Theatre Crafts, P.O. Box 630, Holmes, PA 19043-0630. (Published annually, this volume contains a listing of over 1,500 products and services for the performing arts.)

General Supply Houses

Lewis Gluck Theatre Effects
152 W. 25th St.
New York, NY 10001

Grand Stage Lighting Co.
630 W. Lake
Chicago, IL 60606

Mutual Hardware Corp.
5-45 49th Ave.
Long Island City, NY 11101

Norcostco, Inc.
3203 N. Highway 100
Minneapolis, MN 55422

Paramount Wire, Inc.
1523 63rd St.
Brooklyn, NY 11219

Sapsis Rigging, Inc.
305 Carson St.
Philadelphia, PA 19128

The Show Dept.
2252 N. Elston Ave.
Chicago, IL 60614

Stein Theatrical Make-Up Co.
430 Broom St.
New York, NY 10013

Tech Theatre, Inc.
P.O. Box 401
Naperville, IL 60540

Theater Services and Supply, Inc.
170 Oval Dr.
Central Islip, NY 11722

Tobin's Lake Studio
2650 Seven Mile Rd.
South Lyon, MI 48178

Upstaging Inc.
2570 United Lane
Elk Grove Village, IL 60007

Westbank Photo Supply Co.
   (special effects)
833 W. Chicago Ave.
Chicago, IL 60622

Western Service & Supply, Inc.
2100 Stout Street
Denver, CO 80201

Rigging and Hardware

Some firms specialize in rigging, curtains, drops, and other special stage hardware.

Peter Albrecht Corp.
325 East Chicago St.
Milwaukee, WI 53202

Becker Studios
2824 W. Taylor St.
Chicago, IL 60612

J. R. Clancy, Inc.
1010 W. Belden Ave.
Syracuse, NY 13204

Grand Stage Lighting
630 W. Lake
Chicago, IL 60606

Merrill Stage Equipment
6520 Westfall Blvd.
Indianapolis, IN 46220

Curtains and Stage Fabrics

Art Drapery Studios Corp.
5520 W. Touhy
Unit M
Skokie, IL 60076

Chicago Scenic Studios, Inc.
1711 W. Fullerton
Chicago, IL 60614

Dazian Inc. (branches in major U.S. cities)
1423 W. 55th St.
New York, NY 10019

Knoxville Scenic Studios
P.O. Box 1029
Knoxville, TN 37901

Lighting Equipment

Most firms carry a full line of lighting equipment, and some offer rental equipment. Those firms marked with * offer complete consultation and engineering services.

American Stage Lighting
13316 North Ave.
New Rochelle, NY 10804

Berky Colortran*
1015 Chestnut
Burbank, CA 91502

Chicago Spotlight
4595 N. Elston Ave.
Chicago, IL 60630

Control Devices
649 Pugsley
Salt Lake City, UT 84103

Decor Electronics Corp.
4711 E. 5th St.
Austin, TX 78702

Electro Controls, Inc.*
2975 South 300 West
Salt Lake City, UT 84115

Electronics Diversified, Inc.
1675 N.W. 216th
Hillsboro, OR 97123

Grand Stage Lighting
630 W. Lake St.
Chicago, IL 60606

Hub Electric Co.*
940 Industrial Dr.
Elmhurst, IL 60126

Kliegl Bros. Lighting*
5 Aerial Way
Syosset, NY 11791

Stage Lighting Distributors
346 West 44th Street
New York, NY 10036

Strand Lighting
20 Bushes Lane
Elmwood Park, NJ 07407

Strong Electric Co.
521 City Park Ave.
Toledo, OH 43607

Superior Electrical Supply*
394 Broadway
New York, NY 10010

Theatre Techniques Associates, Inc.*
P.O. Box 335
Cornwall-on-the-Hudson, NY 12520

Universal Theatre Supply
1245 Adams St.
Boston, MA 02124

Lighting Media

(Plastic & gelatine) See also General Supply Houses.

Barbizon Electrical Co., Inc.
426 West 55th St.
New York, NY 10019

Rosco Laboratories, Inc.
36 Bush Ave.
Port Chester, NY 10573

Paint

See also General Supply Houses. (Check local dealers for casein colors.)

Gothic Color Co.
727 Washington St.
New York, NY 10014

Day-Glo Color Corp.
303 Wilson Ave.
Newark, NJ 07105

Roscopaint
Rosco Laboratories
36 Bush Ave.
Port Chester, NY 10573

Sound Effects Recordings & Tapes

See also General Supply Houses.

Dramatists Play Service
440 Park Ave. South
New York, NY 10016

II Brothers Music
7005 S. Pulaski
Chicago, IL 60629

Thomas J. Valentino, Inc.
150 West 46th St.
New York, NY 10036

Theatre Sound Systems

Includes companies having intercom as well as full sound systems.

Auditronics, Inc.
297 Summit St.
Memphis, TN 38104

David Clark Co., Inc.
370 Franklin St.
Worcester, MA 01604

Terry Hanley Audio Systems, Inc.
329 Elm St.
Cambridge, MA 02139

Intercom Systems
1111-17th St.
San Francisco, CA 94107

R. J. Recording and Sound
530 Lark
Geneva, IL 60184

The Show Dept.
2252 N. Elston Ave.
Chicago, IL 60614

II Brothers Music
7005 S. Pulaski
Chicago, IL 60629

Performance Evaluation Forms: Blackline Masters

The following forms may be photocopied for classroom use. Evaluation forms are provided for peer and teacher assessment of individual performance, covering the individual actor's stage performance, vocal performance, and dramatic scene interpretation.

Property Plot/Checklist

Costume Plot/Checklist

Makeup Plot/Checklist

Worksheet for Developing a Character

Physical Interpretation of a Character—Peer Evaluation

Vocal Interpretation of a Character—Peer Evaluation

Final Evaluation of a Performance

Miscellaneous Teacher Evaluation Forms

Property Plot/Checklist

Props, because they are often so numerous, frequently cause problems. Early in rehearsal substitutes need to be used so that actors don't expect props to materialize from or disappear into thin air. The prop crew should do a property plot that lists every prop used in each scene, and clearly notes its source and destination.

ACT I, Scene 1

Prop	Source	Destination
_____	prop table	left onstage
_____	_____	carried off and returned to prop table
_____	preset onstage	_____
_____	_____	consumed/destroyed (to be redone each night)
_____	assigned to actor	_____

Costume Plot/Checklist

As the costume crew surveys what needs to be constructed, pulled and rented, they must know what each character needs. As the crew makes final decisions, it is helpful to rely on a costume plot which, scene by scene, lists each character and what each is to wear.

ACT I, Scene 1

Character	**Costume**	**Accessories**	**Notes**
_____	Must be specific. Also note if something is underdressed—e.g., the dress worn in scene 2 is under a bathrobe	e.g., shoes, hats, gloves	e.g., if a costume is to be torn onstage and must be rerigged each night
_____	_____	_____	_____
	_____	_____	_____
	_____	_____	_____

Makeup Plot/Checklist

When the makeup crew assembles what is needed for each character, they will find it helpful to have a detailed makeup plot. They should list the specific bases, shadows and powders to be used on each character. For character, age, or fantastic makeup, the makeup crew may find it helpful to draw a paint-by-number sketch of the character's face.

ACTOR _____

CHARACTER _____

PLAY _____

BASE _____

EYE SHADOW _____

ROUGE _____

HIGHLIGHTER _____

SHADOW _____

POWDER _____

BRUSHES/SPONGES _____

PROSTHESES (nose putty, scars, etc.) _____

_____

CREPE HAIR (mustaches, beards, eyebrows, etc.) _____

_____

WIGS AND HAIRPIECES _____

_____

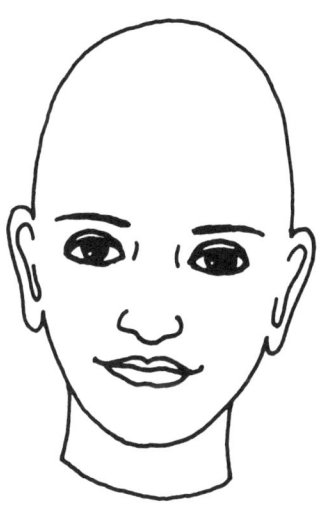

Worksheet for Developing a Character

Often when students have trouble with character development, they can find answers by studying the script and thinking about a few key questions.

1. What is the character's name? Is there any special symbolism or significance associated with the name?

2. What is the character's function in the play? Map out his or her relationships with other characters. Who are his or her other relatives, friends, romantic interests, rivals, and adversaries?

3. What is the age of the character? How does his or her age affect relationships with others in the play? Is he or she looked to for wisdom and respected? Is he or she looked down upon and isolated or regarded as a peer?

4. What is the character's intellectual capacity? How intelligent is he or she compared to other characters onstage? Is the character well-educated? Street-smart? Intuitive?

5. What is the character's background? Is he or she typical of the place and time of the play, or is there something about the character that makes him or her an outsider? To what social class does he or she belong? Was he or she born into this class or has fortune changed the character's life?

6. What physical features distinguish the character. Does he or she have any physical infirmity, or is the character blessed with robust good health? Are any physical attributes commented upon by the character or by those around him or her?

7. Does the character have any personality quirks? How does he or she ordinarily behave? Does his or her behavior remain consistent in times of joy or stress? How does the character's personality change during the course of the play?

8. What beliefs, morals, and aspirations motivate the character? What is the character's major goal in the play? What stands in his or her way? Does the character ultimately achieve his or her goal?

9. List ten adjectives that sum up the essence of the character.

10. Choose one line of dialogue by or about the character that you feel encapsulates him or her.

©National Textbook Company

Physical Interpretation of a Character—
Peer Evaluation Form

Actor _____

Character _____

Play _____

	Excellent	Good	Needs Work
1. Actor's stance and movement are consistent with character's age and physical condition.			
2. Actor's physicalization displays personality and attitudes of the character.			
3. Actor's movements are consistent with the character's social class and time period (i.e., social norms).			
4. Actor's facial expressions contribute to characterization rather than distract from it.			
5. Actor's gestures and stage business contribute to characterization rather than distract from it.			
6. Actor's characterization remains physically consistent throughout the play.			
7. Actor remains in character and properly focused throughout the play.			

Areas in which actor was especially effective:

Areas in which you might suggest improvement:

©National Textbook Company

Vocal Interpretation of a Character—
Peer Evaluation Form

Actor _____

Character _____

Play _____

	Excellent	Good	Needs Work
1. **Articulation** Actor was clearly understood with no unintelligible lines.			
2. **Pitch/Rate** Actor used good variety in pitch and rate, appropriate to the character.			
3. **Volume** Actor could be heard throughout the house, even when modulating volume in character.			
4. **Pauses/Emphasis** Actor effectively used pauses and inflection to convey emotion and interpret character.			
5. **Dialect** If the actor used a stage dialect, it was believable and consistent.			
6. **Consistency** If the actor developed a unique character voice, the voice was employed consistently.			

Areas in which actor was especially effective:

Areas in which you might suggest improvement:

Final Evaluation of a Performance

1. Was the play appropriate for its intended audience? Why? Why not?

2. Were the style and intent of the play clearly understood and consistently carried out? If not, what and where were the specific problems?

3. Was the play cast so that all characters were convincing? If not, what and where were the specific problems?

4. Did all actors convincingly portray their characters? If not, where were their interpretations flawed? How would you have changed the interpretation?

5. Did the sets and lighting convincingly create the desired illusion onstage? If not, what changes would have been beneficial?

6. Were the technical aspects of the show efficiently executed? If there were technical problems, what adaptations might have been made to solve the problems?

7. Did costuming and makeup enhance characterization?

8. If the play was a period drama, were there any apparent anachronisms? How did these affect your perception of the play?

9. Did the pacing of the play allow for proper exposition without plodding or dragging?

10. Did the audience seem to appreciate the performance?

11. How would you rate the show? Would you recommend it to a friend?

Vocal Performance—Teacher Evaluation Form

Performer _____ Grade _____

Selection _____

Clarity	Excellent	Good	Need More
Rate	Excellent	Good	Need More
Pitch	Excellent	Good	Need More
Pauses	Excellent	Good	Need More
Volume	Excellent	Good	Need More
Force	Excellent	Good	Need More
Timbre	Excellent	Good	Need More
Emphasis	Excellent	Good	Need More

Comments:

Scene Interpretation—Teacher Evaluation Form

Performer _____ Grade _____

Selection _____

Vocal Suggestion of Character

Pitch and Timbre	Excellent	Very Good	Average	Poor
Rate and Pauses	Excellent	Very Good	Average	Poor
Volume, Force, and Emphasis	Excellent	Very Good	Average	Poor

Physical Suggestion of Character

Tone, Posture, and Stance	Excellent	Very Good	Average	Poor
Gestures, Facial Expression	Excellent	Very Good	Average	Poor
Character Placement	Excellent	Very Good	Average	Poor
Suggestion of Action	Excellent	Very Good	Average	Poor

Overall Success of Performance

Understanding of Selection	Excellent	Very Good	Average	Poor
Communication with Audience	Excellent	Very Good	Average	Poor

Comments:

NTC SPEECH AND THEATRE BOOKS

Speech Communication
ACTIVITIES FOR EFFECTIVE COMMUNICATION, LiSacchi
THE BASICS OF SPEECH, Galvin, Cooper, & Gordon
CONTEMPORARY SPEECH, HopKins & Whitaker
DYNAMICS OF SPEECH, Myers & Herndon
GETTING STARTED IN PUBLIC SPEAKING, Prentice & Payne
LISTENING BY DOING, Galvin
LITERATURE ALIVE! Gamble & Gamble
MEETINGS: RULES & PROCEDURES, Pohl
PERSON TO PERSON, Galvin & Book
PUBLIC SPEAKING TODAY! Prentice & Payne
SELF-AWARENESS, Ratliffe & Herman
SPEAKING BY DOING, Buys, Sill, & Beck

Theatre
ACTING AND DIRECTING, Grandstaff
THE BOOK OF CUTTINGS FOR ACTING & DIRECTING, Cassady
THE BOOK OF SCENES FOR ACTING PRACTICE, Cassady
THE DYNAMICS OF ACTING, Snyder & Drumsta
AN INTRODUCTION TO MODERN ONE-ACT PLAYS, Cassady
AN INTRODUCTION TO THEATRE AND DRAMA, Cassady & Cassady
NTC's DICTIONARY OF THEATRE AND DRAMA TERMS, Mobley
PLAY PRODUCTION TODAY! Beck et al.
STAGECRAFT, Beck

For a current catalog and information about our complete line of language arts books, write:
National Textbook Company,
a division of NTC Publishing Group
4255 West Touhy Avenue
Lincolnwood (Chicago), Illinois 60646-1975 U.S.A.